Heaven's Her
Jesus Calms A Storm

To: Emery & Charlotte
Fr: Grandma Pat

PEOPLE ARE TALKING ABOUT *Jesus Calms A Storm*

Jesus Calms A Storm delivers a wonderful message, underpinned by the story layering, beginning with God's Word and culminating with Jesus's calming of the storm. The artful and skillfully constructed scaffold of cumulative phrases reinforces the story, built page by page through beautiful illustrations as the story unfolds. The prayer on each page offers reassurance to the reader and brings home the message that God is with us when we're afraid.

—**John Alexander**, Children's book author. Newest release, *The Christmas Gift*.

HEAVEN'S HEROES
Jesus Calms A Storm

Kristin Lehr

Illustrated by Alicia Berry

Copyright Notice

Jesus Calms A Storm

First edition. Copyright © 2019 by Kristin Lehr. The information contained in this book is the intellectual property of Kristin Lehr and is governed by United States and International copyright laws. All rights reserved. No part of this publication, either text or image, may be used for any purpose other than personal use. Therefore, reproduction, modification, storage in a retrieval system, or retransmission, in any form or by any means, electronic, mechanical, or otherwise, for reasons other than personal use, except for brief quotations for reviews or articles and promotions, is strictly prohibited without prior written permission by the publisher. This book is a work of Biblical fiction.

Cover and Interior Design: Derinda Babcock

Editor(s): Derinda Babcock, Deb Haggerty

Illustrated by: Alicia Berry

Author Represented by WordWise Media Services

Library Cataloging Data

Names: Lehr, Kristin (Kristin Lehr)

Jesus Calms A Storm / Kristin Lehr

40 p. 21.6 cm × 21.6 cm (8.5 in × 8.5 in.)

Description: PUBLISHED BY: Elk Lake Publishing, Inc., 35 Dogwood Dr., Plymouth, MA 02360, 2019

Identifiers: ISBN-13: 978-1-951080-55-6 (trade hardcover) | 978-1-951080-56-3 (trade paperback) | 978-1-951080-57-0 (POD)

Key Words: Children ages 4 to 8, Picture book, Christian, Bible story, Spiral learning, Read together book, Miracles of Jesus

LCCN: 2019952377 Fiction

Author's Dedication

Connor

There will be times when you're scared
and don't know where to turn.
Remember the one who commands
the wind and the waves. Look up!
Psalm 56:3 "When I am afraid I put my trust in you."

I love you and I am proud of you!

Mark 4:30

The Parable of the Mustard Seed

30 Again he said, "What shall we say the kingdom of God is like, or what parable shall we use to describe it? 31 It is like a mustard seed, which is the smallest of all seeds on earth. 32 Yet when planted, it grows and becomes the largest of all garden plants, with such big branches that the birds can perch in its shade."

33 With many similar parables Jesus spoke the word to them, as much as they could understand. 34 He did not say anything to them without using a parable. But when he was alone with his own disciples, he explained everything.

Jesus Calms the Storm

35 That day when evening came, he said to his disciples, "Let us go over to the other side." 36 Leaving the crowd behind, they took him along, just as he was, in the boat. There were also other boats with him. 37 A furious squall came up, and the waves broke over the boat, so that it was nearly swamped. 38 Jesus was in the stern, sleeping on a cushion. The disciples woke him and said to him, "Teacher, don't you care if we drown?"

39 He got up, rebuked the wind and said to the waves, "Quiet! Be still!" Then the wind died down and it was completely calm.

40 He said to his disciples, "Why are you so afraid? Do you still have no faith?"

41 They were terrified and asked each other, "Who is this? Even the wind and the waves obey him!"

Jesus Restores a Demon-Possessed Man

5 They went across the lake to the region of the Gerasenes.[a] 2 When Jesus got out of the boat, a man with an impure spirit came from the tombs to meet him. 3 This man lived in the tombs, and no one could bind him anymore, not even with a chain. 4 For he had often been chained hand and foot, but he tore the chains apart and broke the irons on his feet. No one was strong enough to subdue him. 5 Night and day among the tombs and in the hills he would cry out and cut himself with stones.

6 When he saw Jesus from a distance, he ran and fell on his knees in front of him. 7 He shouted at the top of his voice, "What do you want with me, Jesus, Son of the Most High God? In God's name don't torture me!" 8 For Jesus had said to him, "Come out of this man, you impure spirit!"

9 Then Jesus asked him, "What is your name?"

"My name is Legion," he replied, "for we are many." 10 And he begged Jesus again and again not to send them out of the area.

11 A large herd of pigs was feeding on the nearby hillside. 12 The demons begged Jesus, "Send us among the pigs; allow us to go into them." 13 He gave them permission, and the impure spirits came out and went into the pigs. The herd, about two thousand in number, rushed down the steep bank into the lake and were drowned.

14 Those tending the pigs ran off and reported this in the town and countryside, and the people went out to see what had happened. 15 When they came to Jesus, they saw the man who had been possessed by the legion of demons, sitting there, dressed and in his right mind; and they were afraid. 16 Those who had seen it told the people what had happened to the demon-possessed man—and told about the pigs as well. 17 Then the people began to plead with Jesus to leave their region.

18 As Jesus was getting into the boat, the man who had been demon-possessed begged to go with him. 19 Jesus did not let him, but said, "Go home to your own people and tell them how much the Lord has done for you, and how he has had mercy on you." 20 So the man went away and began to tell in the Decapolis[b] how much Jesus had done for him. And all the people were amazed.

Jesus Raises a Dead Girl and Heals a Sick Woman

21 When Jesus had again crossed over by boat to the other side of the lake, a large crowd gathered around him while he was by the lake. 22 Then one of the synagogue leaders, named Jairus, came, and when he saw Jesus, he fell at his feet. 23 He pleaded earnestly with him, "My little daughter is dying. Please come and put your hands on her so that she will be healed and live." 24 So Jesus went with him. A large crowd followed and pressed around him. 25 And a woman was there who had been subject to bleeding for twelve years. 26 She had suffered a great deal under the care of many doctors and had spent all she had, yet instead of getting better she grew worse. 27 When she heard about Jesus, she came up behind him in the crowd and touched his cloak, 28 because she thought, "If I just touch his clothes, I will be healed." 29 Immediately her bleeding stopped and she felt in her body that she was freed from her suffering.

30 At once Jesus realized that power had gone out from him. He turned around in the crowd and asked, "Who touched my clothes?"

31 "You see the people crowding against you," his disciples

This is God's word.

Dear God, thank you for being with me when I'm afraid.

This is Jesus preaching God's word.

Dear God, thank you for being with me when I'm afraid.

This is the crowd listening to Jesus
preach God's word.

Dear God, thank you for being with me when I'm afraid.

This is the shore, sandy and shaded,
where the crowd listens to Jesus
preach God's word.

Dear God, thank you for being with me when I'm afraid.

This is the boat that's kept afloat
which bobs near the shore, sandy and shaded,
where the crowd listens to Jesus
preach God's word.

Dear God, thank you for being with me when I'm afraid.

These are his friends, we call them disciples,
who sit in the boat that's kept afloat
which bobs near the shore, sandy and shaded,
where the crowd listens to Jesus
preach God's word.

Dear God, thank you for being with me when I'm afraid.

Jesus needs rest and follows his friends,
we call them disciples,
who sit in the boat that's kept afloat
which bobs near the shore, sandy and shaded,
where the crowd listens to Jesus
preach God's word.

Dear God, thank you for being with me when I'm afraid.

This is our Savior, he's in a deep sleep,
so tired from talking, no need to count sheep.
He needs to recover and rest is what's best,
so he follows his friends,
we call them disciples,
who sit in the boat that's kept afloat
which bobs near the shore, sandy and shaded,
where the crowd listens to Jesus
preach God's word.

Dear God, thank you for being with me when I'm afraid.

This is a storm, some call it a squall,
that starts quick and strong, as his pals start to bawl
while our Savior, he's in a deep sleep,
so tired from talking, no need to count sheep.
He needs to recover and rest is what's best,
so he follows his friends,
we call them disciples,
who sit in the boat that's kept afloat
which bobs near the shore, sandy and shaded,
where the crowd listens to Jesus
preach God's word.

Dear God, thank you for being with me when I'm afraid.

"Help us!" they fuss in the eye of the storm
some call it a squall that starts quick and strong
as his pals start to bawl while our Savior is quiet
and in a deep sleep, so tired from talking,
no need to count sheep.
He needs to recover and rest is what's best,
so he follows his friends, we call them disciples,
into the boat that's kept afloat
which bobs near the shore, sandy and shaded,
where the crowd listens to Jesus
preach God's word.

Dear God, thank you for being with me when I'm afraid.

Crack! rumbles the thunder as waves
pull them under.
"Help us!" they fuss in the eye of the storm
some call it a squall that starts quick and strong
as his pals start to bawl while our Savior is quiet
and in a deep sleep, so tired from talking,
no need to count sheep.
He needs to recover and rest is what's best,
so he follows his friends, we call them disciples,
into the boat that's kept afloat
which bobs near the shore, sandy and shaded,
where the crowd listens to Jesus
preach God's word.

Dear God, thank you for being with me when I'm afraid.

Friends shake and shiver as they try to deliver a message to God,
while *Crack!* rumbles the thunder as waves pull them under.
"Help us!" they fuss in the eye of the storm
some call it a squall that starts quick and strong
as his pals start to bawl while our Savior is quiet
and in a deep sleep, so tired from talking,
no need to count sheep.
He needs to recover and rest is what's best,
so he follows his friends, we call them disciples,
into the boat that's kept afloat
which bobs near the shore, sandy and shaded,
where the crowd listens to Jesus
preach God's word.

Dear God, thank you for being with me when I'm afraid.

Jesus awakes and steps toward the bow.
Friends shake and shiver as they try to deliver a message to God,
while *Crack!* rumbles the thunder as waves pull them under.
"Help us!" they fuss in the eye of the storm
some call it a squall that starts quick and strong
as his pals start to bawl while our Savior is quiet
and in a deep sleep, so tired from talking,
no need to count sheep.
He needs to recover and rest is what's best,
so he follows his friends, we call them disciples,
into the boat that's kept afloat
which bobs near the shore, sandy and shaded,
where the crowd listens to Jesus
preach God's word.

Dear God, thank you for being with me when I'm afraid.

"Quiet. Be still!" the Messiah demands,
and the wind and the waves obey his command.
As Jesus awakes and steps toward the bow,
friends shake and shiver as they try to deliver a message to God,
while *Crack!* rumbles the thunder as waves pull them under.
"Help us!" they fuss in the eye of the storm
some call it a squall that starts quick and strong
as his pals start to bawl while our Savior is quiet
and in a deep sleep, so tired from talking,
no need to count sheep.
He needs to recover and rest is what's best,
so he follows his friends, we call them disciples,
into the boat that's kept afloat
which bobs near the shore, sandy and shaded,
where the crowd listens to Jesus
preach God's word.

Dear God, thank you for being with me when I'm afraid.

The sea becomes calm, a lesson to all,
Do what he says, he's in charge of us all.
"Quiet. Be still!" the Messiah demands,
and the wind and the waves obey his command.
As Jesus awakes and steps toward the bow,
friends shake and shiver as they try to deliver a message to God,
while *Crack!* rumbles the thunder as waves pull them under.
"Help us!" they fuss in the eye of the storm
some call it a squall that starts quick and strong
as his pals start to bawl while our Savior is quiet
and in a deep sleep, so tired from talking, no need to count sheep.
He needs to recover and rest is what's best,
so he follows his friends, we call them disciples,
into the boat that's kept afloat
which bobs near the shore, sandy and shaded,
where the crowd listens to Jesus
preach God's word.

Dear God, thank you for being with me when I'm afraid.

The friends are amazed and will follow God's son
for all of their days as the sea becomes calm, a lesson to all,
Do what he says, he's in charge of us all.
"Quiet. Be still!" the Messiah demands,
and the wind and the waves obey his command.
As Jesus awakes and steps toward the bow,
friends shake and shiver as they try to deliver a message to God,
while *Crack!* rumbles the thunder as waves pull them under.
"Help us!" they fuss in the eye of the storm
some call it a squall that starts quick and strong
as his pals start to bawl while our Savior is quiet
and in a deep sleep, so tired from talking, no need to count sheep.
He needs to recover and rest is what's best,
so he follows his friends, we call them disciples,
into the boat that's kept afloat
which bobs near the shore, sandy and shaded,
where the crowd listens to Jesus
preach God's word.

Dear God, thank you for being with me when I'm afraid.

Inspired from Psalm 46:10 Be still and know that I am God.

ABOUT THE AUTHOR

Dr. Kristin Lehr, author of *The Squirrel Family Acorn*, lives in Indiana with her husband and three sons. Her favorite thing is to spend time with family and friends. Her guilty pleasures are shopping and watching reality TV. Kristin enjoys a wonderful career as the Director of Children's Ministry at Zionsville Presbyterian Church in Zionsville, Indiana.

Stay tuned for the next exciting book in the *Heaven's Heroes* series…"

ABOUT THE ILLUSTRATOR

ALICIA BERRY grew up in Westfield, Indiana, and is currently a student at Columbus College of Art and Design. Studying illustration, she works with both traditional and digital media to create her artworks. She spends her summers at Lake Cumberland in Kentucky where she enjoys houseboating and waterskiing. Alicia is unsure what the future holds for her but has high hopes for this coffee-fueled artistic journey.

Made in the USA
Lexington, KY
28 October 2019